OMFG!

Why Parents Should (Still) Never Text!

Oscar Harris

BLACK & WHITE PUBLISHING

First published 2016
by Black & White Publishing Ltd
29 Ocean Drive, Edinburgh EH6 6JL

1 3 5 7 9 10 8 6 4 2   16 17 18 19

ISBN: 978 1 78530 062 2

A CIP catalogue record for this book is available from the British Library.

Typeset by 3btype.com
Printed and bound by CPI Group (UK) Ltd, Croydon, CR0 4YY

OMFG!

Contents

Text Message   Send

Dad

I'm watching the Bobbin. Billabong Baggage is the best!

The Huddle

The hobbies

The Bobbin

The Huddle

lol damn this phone!

Billabong baggage

I give up

Billboard baggage

Seriously iFail?

DAD

Text Message
Send

Dad
How long til you get here?
God says 20 minutes.
I trust him.
Just in case though, what does GPS say?
. . . I hate you.
Text Message
Send

Dad

Beth I wanted to let you know Zoe is having a tummy ache and is lying on the sofa

She died

What????

Doesn't have a fever

That's a typo right?????

Sorry that was terrible I hate messaging

Yes so sorry

Oh jeez that damn near gave me a heart attack!

Text Message   Send

WHY PARENTS SHOULD (STILL) NEVER TEXT

Dad

Did you move my yoghurt?

No

Looks like the fridge has a case of the Paranormal Activia

Text Message   Send

Dad
Printer not working, I tried the usual stuff – unplugging, beating it, put my balls on it and prayed?
Hmm that usually works.
Text Message
Send

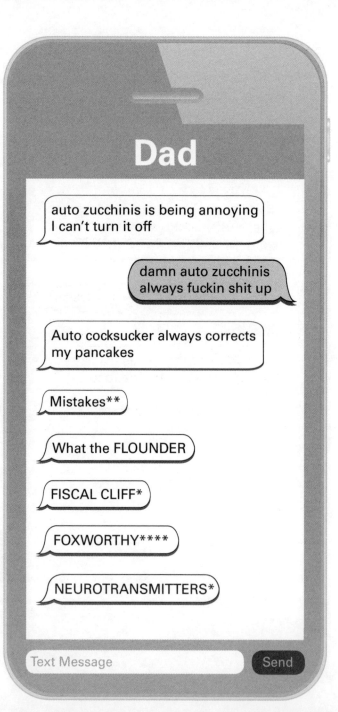

Dad
This is Jesus this is my new number ✪
Jessi
I was shocked that Jesus felt like I was a close enough friend to give me his number . . .
Text Message
Send

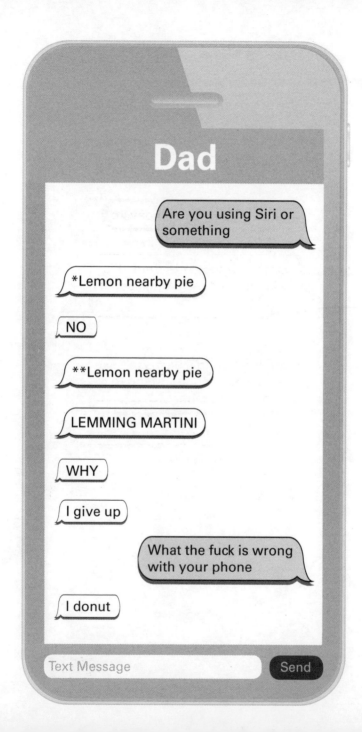

Dad

Xo have a great day today xo

I want to teach you to drink this weekend. Trust me, I think you'll be great at it!

OMG DRIVE! Not drink!

I was so excited for a moment.

You wish.

Text Message   Send

WHY PARENTS SHOULD (STILL) NEVER TEXT

Dad
Are u coming home for dinner?
I'm sorry I just came from the storm coming home like right now sorry
No worries
Okay I love you should be able Hoopohu prints pop poop poop poop be do ostrich feathers in my butt to getting Odinga being a boo
Eh?
It's not just me, Siri thinks u mumble too
Text Message
Send

Dad

I want to buy a pet bird for mum. Maybe a parrot.

Oh that's cool.

When I was in my 20s I had a COCKATTACK.

Oh didn't we all.

Ahhh hahaha Cockatoo, even!

How many times have you typed cockattack!?

Too many, apparently!!

Text Message   Send

WHY PARENTS SHOULD (STILL) NEVER TEXT

Dad
where is granny I thought she was going to be here for Christmas?
Grandma is in the grave.
what grave? what are you saying?
Oops sorry garage
Oh autocorrect
Text Message
Send

Dad are you home

yea whats up

Gonna swing by and grab your balls if that's ok

i don't think i'm down with that

Shit, your van. Def don't need your schwetty balls

well that's good to know. i'm here until 3 so come before then.

Text Message

Send

WHY PARENTS SHOULD (STILL) NEVER TEXT

Dad

Ps. For Mother's Day Mum wants a racist cock from Ikea. It's like £65 I was thinking we could all go in on that as well.

*ragcock

I must be spelling it wrong. It's like a crafting cart.

That's so funny!!!!!!!!!

Text Message   Send

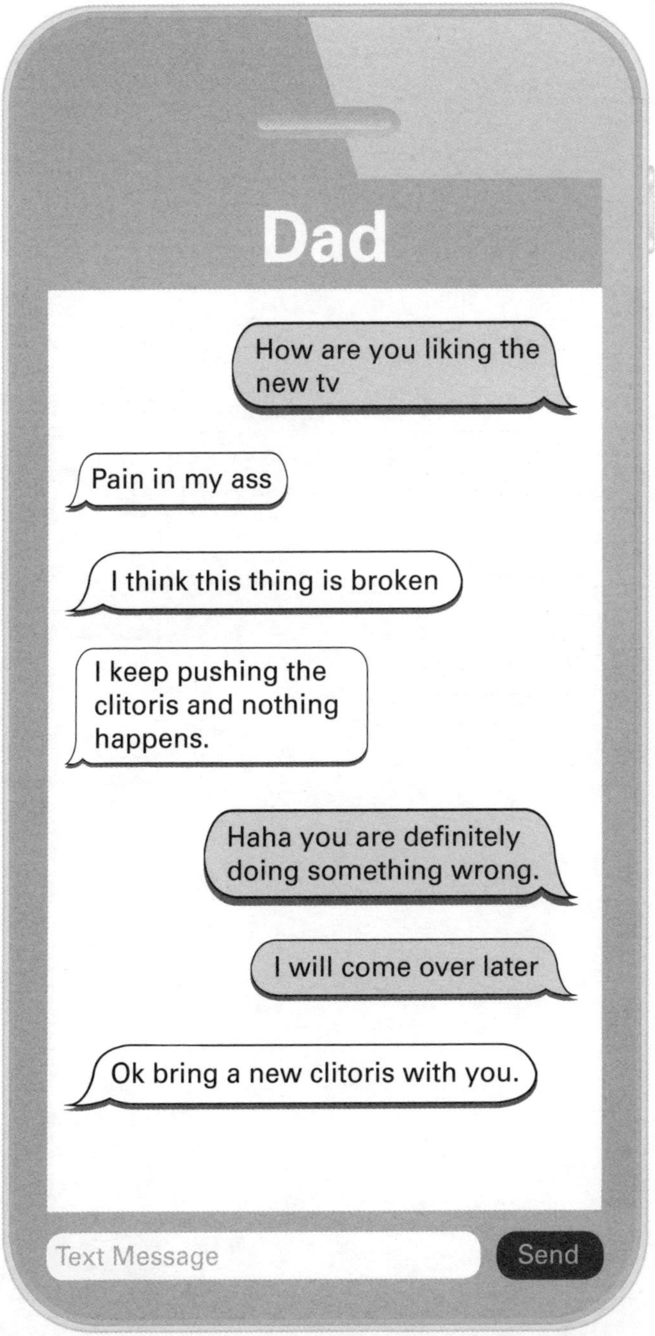
Dad
How are you liking the new tv
Pain in my ass
I think this thing is broken
I keep pushing the clitoris and nothing happens.
Haha you are definitely doing something wrong.
I will come over later
Ok bring a new clitoris with you.
Text Message
Send

Dad

I just tried calling mum.
Is she with you?

She's in the garden

Pantydroppin

*Planting. I am sure
her pants are still on.

LMAO! Matt's been
borrowing your phone,
hasn't he?

Yup.

Text Message   Send

Good evening kind father

What's up, my little gold digger?

Text Message　　　Send

Dad

If you're home, your mum said for you to take the baby out of the freezer and defrost it for brunch today . . .

. . . uhh baby? Do we have a sibling I don't know about? If so do you think the freezer is an appropriate place to keep it?

*bacon not baby!! Yes it would be inappropriate to keep it in there!

Text Message   Send

Dad

Hi, this is Randy. I saw your penis for sale on EBay?

If so I would like to bring my son to give it a test drive tonight sometime.

Hi Randy, I'm selling a prius. Is that what you meant?

YES!!! Apologies, new phone

Well it's EBay. You never know.

Text Message   Send

WHY PARENTS SHOULD (STILL) NEVER TEXT

Dad

Met your sister's new rescue dog. It has HUGE balls. Now I'm thinking I never want to sit on the couch at her house again.

Dad. How do I even reply to that!?

I dunno. If you go, bring febreeze.

Text Message   Send

Dad
Love you that's it send Siri send it Siri are you on crack send the message to her
Text Message
Send

Dad

Daaaaad when can I get a new car?

When you sell your old one for lots more money than we bought it for

Try this

Polo for sale – mint condition!!

Text Message   Send

Dad

I'm watching a movie

What movie?

It's about a man's wife who is brutally murdered by a serial killer and his son left physically disabled. In a twisted turn of events his son is kidnapped and the dad has to track and chase the kidnapper thousands of miles with the help of a mentally disabled woman.

Oh wow

It's finding nemo

Holy fucking shit

Text Message   Send

Dad

Goin out with your mother. See you later

Wait how am I supposed to get in the house?

Magic. You put your cock in the hole and turn it. Voila

Hahaha fail dad

Key you wise ass. I'm sure you are familiar with putting tiny things in holes.

Ooh burn

Text Message | Send

Mum

What did you want for dinner tonight?

Rainbow stew lol

Chicken vaginas n butch gobbler pirates

I mean chick vaginas and bitchgobblet potatoes

Omfg I hate this . . . chicken fajitas and buttered potatoes

N corn

Wtf are you talking about lmao

MUM

Text Message | Send

Mum
Hello Drew if you are not busy I would love it if you could munch my box later
MUNCH my box like talked about on Monday
fiddlesticks
Uh . . .
m u l c h my garden box please thanks love mum
hahaha wow
Text Message
Send

Mum

Daddy broke his arm

OHMYGOD is he ok??? What happened

He slipped and fell off the black dick.

The black dick I mean

The back dick

Why is dad riding black dicks? LMAO do you mean back deck

Yes black dick. Passed out now on pain pills.

Text Message   Send

WHY PARENTS SHOULD (STILL) NEVER TEXT

Mum

How are you mum?

I am not mum
I am golly
You are precious she's
southbound

Southbound?

Holy typos/autocorrect,
batman

What did you mean?

??

I am gollum
You are precioussssssssssssssss

Text Message   Send

Mum
Please don't forget to bring the strawberry jam
Ok. Should I bring the peanut butter too?
No. Just the strawberry and the vagina flavoured cupcakes that aunt Emily made earlier
I mean vagina
VAGINA!
Goddammit! V A N I L L A
Text Message
Send

Mum
Do you think Obama will declare war on diarrhea?
I really don't think that's a priority right now . . .
You're crazy. We live on the coast. We can be hit at any moment
Um, try Imodium or Pepto
Huh?
Oh! North Korea! Not diarrhea.
Text Message
Send

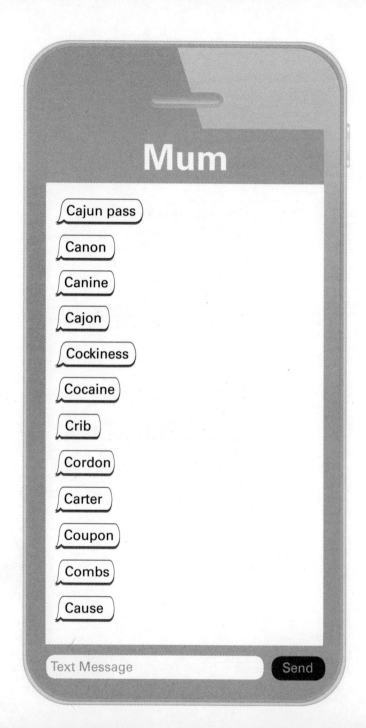

Mum

I am at Homebase. do you need more paint.

Yes I need prob 5 more litres.

what is the colour, I forgot the name

Dulux 7708-7 CHOCOLATE SHART

I just asked for that and the guy laughed at me for like 5 minutes.

Omg omg it's chocolate sparkle!!! I am LMAO

Sorry

Text Message   Send

WHY PARENTS SHOULD (STILL) NEVER TEXT

Mum

What does Sam need for his birthday besides that shirt?

Darth badger sleep pillow for his bed?

I have no idea what that is.

Just looks like his helmet as a fuzzy pillow.

Mum. Reread.

Now I'm crying in the supermarket.

I'm crying in the kitchen.

Darth badger don't care.

Text Message — Send

Mum

Need anything from the supermarket?

Yes! Please bring me home a huge mountain jew!

A Mountain Jew? I don't think I've ever seen one of those at Tesco!

HAHAHA I love mountain jews. So rugged,

But I'd take a mountain dew if you ran across those, too.

Text Message   Send

Mum

You're going to herpangina alarm for awhile are you jealous

Are ha ha eureka is a dog

Oh my gosh Siri is paying. I'm going to that Portland character in bellyache out

I give up

I have no clue what you are saying.

I'm going to toowong parents room are you jealous?

Text Message   Send

Mum

I want to do yoga today

Then do so!

I feel so much better after I do yoda

Yoga! Lmfao I spit my coffee

Hahahahahahhahaah friskyyyy

Sleep with yoda I do not lolol

Text Message   Send

56

Mum

Waiting for prescription to be ready.

You are all you got it for me is another Bengali you all Landerset and many more on the wall and her mum and her mum I'll balance for my back and you are gay

My phone made this message for you. I'm not crazy . . .

Maybe you're not, but your phone is! What was that?

Text Message · Send

Mum

> I haaaaate April. This month is rainy and disgusting.

It will be over soon! April showers bring May flatulence!

> Oh because thats something to look forward to!

lol *flowers

Every month is flatulence month where I live. Have you met your father?

Text Message | Send

Mum

how are you feeling today?

Omg I'm taking Benadryl and drinking hot tea when I get home. Tomorrow morning I'm making Chuck Norris soup in the crockpot for when I get home.

Chuck Norris soup

Shit. No. While I'm sure Chuck Norris soup has incredible healing power, I'm out of the main ingredient. I will try chicken noodle instead.

Text Message   Send

Mum

I think i need to face the fact that I need to upgrade to a bigger pussy

What?

Mine is a disaster all the time. It really doesn't have enough compartments to keep it organised well enough.

So you mean purse?

. . . Yes.

Text Message   Send

Wads up

Witch pat

What the actual fork

Dammit apple let me be racist!!

Rapist

0MG. R E A L

Damn you ass cork

0.0 AUTOCORRECT!!!!

I'm done

Text Message   Send

Mum
how's school going
Oh it's great! I just had the best weed of my life.
I MEAN WEEK!!! Not weed. I swear.
Sounds great but don't tell your father
Text Message
Send

Mum
Ma do you have the key to dads jeep? He wants me to get the oil changed.
Oh yes it's here in my vag. Come and get it please.
I mean it is sitting in my vag
My b a g
Omg. That's a relief because dad was about to go get his own damn oil changed.
Text Message
Send

Mum

We are out of white whore milk. Can you pick some up? I want to eat my coco puffs!

Really, Steve Jobs?

Sory mum it autocorrected whole to whore.

Oh ok who is Steve Jobs?

Text Message   Send

WHY PARENTS SHOULD (STILL) NEVER TEXT

Mum

What up foo

Not much. Sorry was busy spraying a mound of anus. Your little brother spilled something sweet on the porch and they were crawling all over the place so I found whe

re they lived and sprayed anus killer in their hole.

ANTS!!! Mound of ants!!!

And Ant killer in their hole wtf wtf wtf

Lmao

Text Message   Send

Mum

> Hey ma

> Question: can I have my cock out at your house on sat?

ANTHONY. That is disgusting. I'm at work. Call your father. You're not being funny.

> Oh my god lol sorry mum

> I wrote cook out.

I raised you better than to talk to people like that.

> IT WAS AUTOCORRECT

Text Message   Send

WHY PARENTS SHOULD (STILL) NEVER TEXT

Mum

Did I tell you dad and I are going on a cruise to the Bahamas in January?

No! Jealous. What cruise line?

Royal Crap ribbons.

Oh god i just laughed so hard I think I broke something.

Text Message   Send

WHY PARENTS SHOULD (STILL) NEVER TEXT

Mum

Everything is okay here, don't worry! Have fun!

Oh, PS, I smelled your panties on the way out. Delightful.

MUM!!! Lmao – Reread your text.

Pansies!!! Oh my gosh.

You're not allowed to text anymore! And get away from my panties! HAHAHAH

Text Message | Send

Mum
Idk I haven't seen it
But I haven't looked
OKAY
Did you see my green calculator yet?
No loser mcloserson
Text Message
Send

Mum
There's a burglar in the house!
OMG CALL THE POLICE GET OUT OF THERE
I'm coming now get out of there
No there's a burglar in the house!!!
I know I'm coming. Mum call the police and get out
There's a S Q U I R E L in the house!!!
A squirrel? Are you kidding me?
Text Message
Send

Mum

Hi Tony it's mum.

I'm going to your house to take my life tonight

Love you

What the hell are you talking about mum are you ok???

Calling you pick up

I'm coming to take my light. That I let you borrow in February.

Wow ok

Text Message   Send

WHY PARENTS SHOULD (STILL) NEVER TEXT

Mum
I have the apple pie and the cherry pie did you need me to bring anything else?
Dad won't be here tonight, we're getting separated.
Canned corn
WHAT????!?
Canned corn
Text Message
Send

Mum
Matthew I won't be home until late
Don't forget to lock your grandmother in the shed overnight.
Call mobile if you need me. Love you.
Text Message
Send

Mum

Don't forget to unload the dishwasher

Did you finish your homework?

We have to go to your grandmother's house for Christmas.

Dad and I talked, we are going to buy you a car next month.

U are??? Omg thank u

No. We're not. I just wanted to make sure you were getting my texts.

That was cruel

Life is cruel

Text Message   Send

Mum

need t shirt for concert that says cougars love 1d

Text Message

Send

Mum

I'm sick :'(the flu is going around at work, wish I were home so you could take care of meeee, miss you

Who is this

Text Message   Send

Mum
Heard you got an iphone! How do you like it?
Massachusetts
Text Message
Send

Mum

Oh est mâle You tirés how long have You been yp

Heat

Tiref

Tired

Up

I need to practice this

Text Message   Send

Mum

How's your day going?

Awful. I have a bad case of the manboobs.

Omg. The MONDAYS!!! Not manboobs. Jesus.

Text Message — Send

Mum

What do u want for dinner?

I'LL TELL YOU WHAT I WANT WHAT I REALLY REALLY WANT

SO TELL ME WHAT YOU WANT WHAT YOU REALLY REALLY WANT

Ahahaha best mum ever. pizza'd be awesome, please.

Text Message   Send

Mum

So, how do you like your new Iphone?

Zesty vessel

That was weird . . . And unresponsive.

Hey dingleberry yeah its grape I lobster all the fetish. Much llamas on dad.

Oops how do I turn off the erection

I won't ask any more questions.

Text Message   Send

Mum

I'm lesbian now.
C u in 10–15 minutes.

LEAVING! I meant leaving
now. Damn autocorrect.

Why r u a lesbian?

Text Message   Send

WHY PARENTS SHOULD (STILL) NEVER TEXT

Mum

So someone told me you sound like an owl.

How's that?

Darn. It didn't work. You were supposed to say 'who?' 😊😊😊

Lol ok

Who?

Never mind. Moment gone.

Text Message   Send

Mum

Do u think u would ever have use for a rock collection? It is a small set with about 50 rocks?

Text Message | Send

Mum

How's it going?

Are u coming home?

I invented a new drink

vitamin water and
raspberry vodka

feeling good

Text Message   Send

Mum

Hi there! Could you take some pics of my son for his graduation yearbook? Maybe this week?

Of course.

Thanks! I will have him call you.

Please be sure to take portraits, and also several testicle shots.

Excuse me? I'm not that kind of photographer lol

Verticle shots! Yikes!!!!!

Text Message   Send

Mum

A reminder we are away for a week tomorrow u are in charge of house no parties be good mam x

Arrived safe & well very warm staying in the shade nice hotel could be cleaner tired now be good no parties mam x

Last supper 2 night daddy sent back soup too cold they said it is supposed to be – eejit! Be good no parties mam x

Flight delayed bloody ryan air will u keep eye on flight teletext page 217? be good no parties mam x

Text Message   Send

Mum

you will be grounded!

Does that mean I get to nap all weekend>

COME HERE NOW! OR U WILL NOT GO TO FB TOMORROW

I don't know if my wife will let me . . .

Sorry! I just realized you are not my son! Who are you?

Daniel. Nice to meet you

you too . . . tell your wife I'm sorry!

It's okay. She actually wants me to apologise for goofing around. Hope you find him.

☺ All good!!!

Have a nice night

Text Message | Send

WHY PARENTS SHOULD (STILL) NEVER TEXT

Mum

> Know that I kept it sexy and know I kept it fun

Ok I will talk 2 u later I think u are trying 2 annoy me!

> There's something that I'm missing, maybe my head for one

Yes I think so!

> Haha, Mam! I'm texting you a Beyonce song

I prefer Adele

Text Message　　Send

Mum

Did you hear about David Bowie very sad chicken for dinner tonight mum xx

Text Message

Send

Mum

You're gamey Leedy his penis Aun tyne hoar

Mum. Read it before you send it.

Call make. Call blow. Call now.

No. It's waaaay more fun this way

Text Message   Send

Mum
Elizabeth did you do something to my phone. Every time I type butt it changes it to butt.
What does it change it to?
butt
That's really strange. Try typing the original word again.
butt
This is great
Text Message
Send

Mum
Game of Thrones is on again tonight at 9 if you want to watch it
Thank you honey but I can't. I'll be in bed. I have to be up at 4am to do a porno at work tomorrow.
Wow mum, Is money that rough? ☺
Not porno! Promo! I don't do pornos at work!
I have to admit, that's a real relief.
Text Message
Send

> **Mum**
>
> I just got to the supermarket
>
> Ok . . .
>
> What size shits do you take?
>
> What!? Mum that's disgusting! Haha
> And large, by the way.
>
> Good grief! This phone! Shirts.

Mum

So what kind of souvenir would you like from San Diego? Something from the zoo? Padres? Beach? Just San Diego? Tshirts? Hat? Stuffed animal?

Surprise me ☺

Ok, stuffed anal it is!!

Stuffed anal!?!!? Ewwwwww

I meant animal. Not anal

That would be a surprise indeed.

Text Message   Send

Mum

I lobe you soo much sweetie. We're at the Olvie Garden! 2-4-1 chardinay!

Drink some water mum

I'm so happy I decided to keep you

Text Message   Send

ADVICE

Mum

Just be careful if they try brainwashing you

Lol how are they going to brainwash me?

If it seems cult like

Mum it's yoga.

I have heard of women leaving their families with little kids

To follow yoga groups?

Text Message   Send

Mum

> Today is miserable and neverending.

If Britney can make it through 2008, you can make it through today, sweetie

> Haha you're so right. Thanks, mum

Text Message | Send

Mum

Remember to eat three pickles for breakfast before you leave. You'll lose weight this time for good.

And it's cheap.

Text Message   Send

Mum

At night club

Should I fist pump?

Oh dear god. No!

Why not?

Oh god mum

Okay I will dance instead???

No not that either

Text Message   Send

Mum

> Mum I need you hurry I cant get out of bed

> Mum someone covered my floor in legos

> MUM!!!!!!!

You will never forget mothers day again will you.

> WOW MUM TOO FAR.

Oh and if you miss school you'll be grounded for a year. Bus gets here in 10 mins GOOD LUCK ;)

Text Message | Send

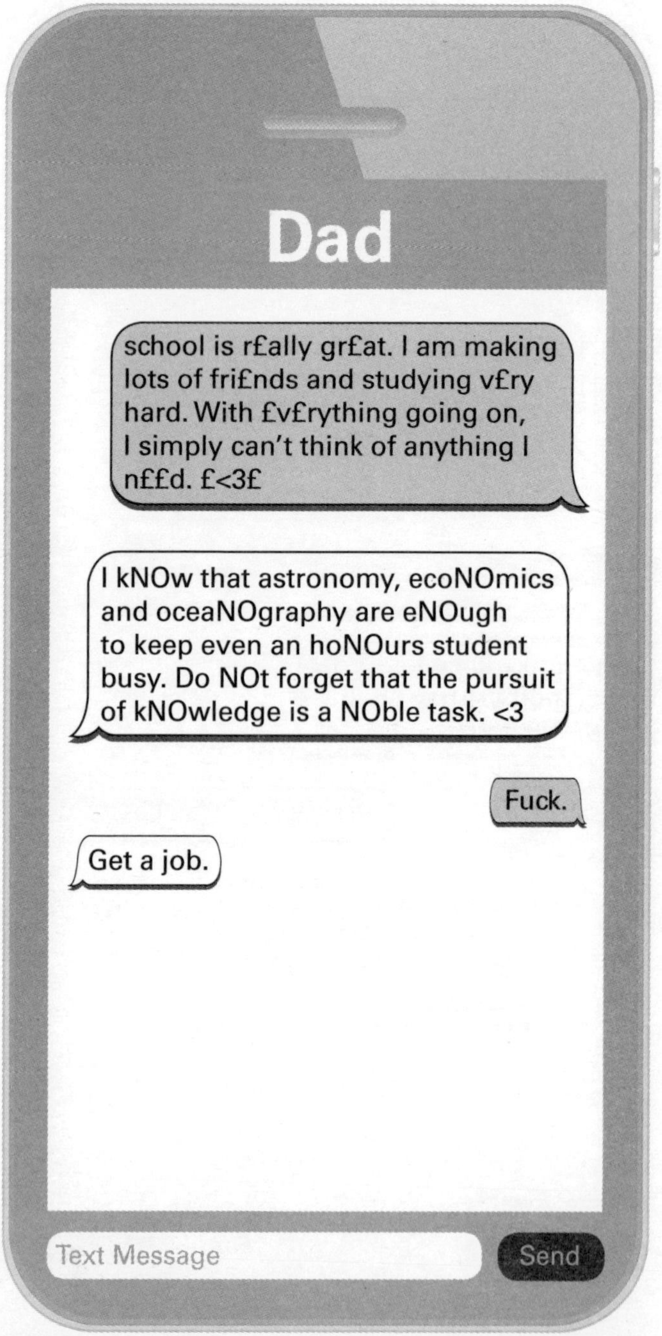
Dad
school is r£ally gr£at. I am making lots of fri£nds and studying v£ry hard. With £v£rything going on, I simply can't think of anything I n££d. £<3£
I kNOw that astronomy, ecoNOmics and oceaNOgraphy are eNOugh to keep even an hoNOurs student busy. Do NOt forget that the pursuit of kNOwledge is a NOble task. <3
Fuck.
Get a job.
Text Message
Send

Dad

Did you know there is a One Direction documentary coming out? It was in my magazine on my flight today. Almost took a pic to send you . . .

Supposed to be full of bare chest moments . . .

Can't wait!!!!!!

Text Message   Send

Dad

> I want to punch her in the eye. With a rusty fork.

> Well this is awkward. I didn't mean to text that to you. Hi dad.

> LOL, hi Katie. DoN't forget to wear gloves, keeps the fingerprints off the fork, even if it IS a rusty one

> My favourite part of this is how you don't even question who it is

> The less I know, the less I can say during the interrogation

Text Message   Send

Mum

> I HATE wearing heels to work. I feel like i'm going to fall over.

Deal with it. They make ur legs look great.

Reminder, exercise ur calf muscles every other day. Unless u want to end up with cankles. It runs in the family.

On your Father's side.

Text Message　　Send

Mum

Are you working Saturday?

Yea and I got asked to do playboy too. I'm gonna do it bc I need the money.

YOU ARE NOT POSING FOR PLAYBOY

OVER MY DEAD EFFING BODY KATHLEEN

Oh wait until your father hears this.

Omfg mum I wrote overtime. Not playboy.

ANSWER PHONE

Text Message   Send

WHY PARENTS SHOULD (STILL) NEVER TEXT

Mum
What does Megan want for her birthday?
get her the skin graft set
She is Hannibal lecter now? WTF
lol I meant the "skin care" set we talked about
Text Message
Send

Mum
What time are you home?
I'm REALLY hungry
Then get some food bitch
Text Message
Send

Mum

Find a cookie. Tell yourself that eating the cookie is a bad idea. Eat the cookie anyway. Regret eating the cookie. Deal with guilt by eating more cookies.

Are you ok?

Text Message   Send

> What should I get Sarah for our first anniversary?

> A candle

> Really, a candle?

> Yes, BITCHES LOVE CANDLES

WHY PARENTS SHOULD (STILL) NEVER TEXT

Mum

Good morning beautiful 😄 xoxo your imaginary boyfriend

Thanks mum . . .

Text Message   Send

RELATIONSHIPS

Mum

> Hey mum I've decided I'm coming out

Oh Micheal, Dad and I always knew you were gay, but I am a tad shocked you texted me! I love you no matter what!

> MUM. I AM NOT GAY. I sent my text before I could finish. I'm coming out to see you and Dad in May!

LOL. We love you no matter what type of coming out you do!

Text Message   Send

Mum

I am divorcing your father! LOL.

Oh god what now mum

He gave me a stiffy for our anniversary last night. Unreal.

A stiffy! Ew mum I don't need to hear about that.

No, a Swiffer. 30 yrs of marriage for a Swiffer.

What is a stiffy

Don't even ask. But its better than a swiffer LOL

Text Message | Send

WHY PARENTS SHOULD (STILL) NEVER TEXT

Mum

Are you on that date?

Yeah can't talk now. I'll let you know how it goes.

Is he cute?

What kind of shirt did he wear?

If you went to that Chinese place, get the egg rolls as starters. They're great.

Ask him if he likes kids

Text Message   Send

Mum
We have a farmer for u
A farmer? For what?
To marry
Text Message
Send

Mum

> Did you like Ben?! He says it was very nice to meet you, the house was lovely and you guys seemed really cool ☺

> Your father and I think he looks like a potato

Text Message · Send

Mum

How did ur date go. Cant wait to hear all about it

It was ok! Food was yummy and he's very nice. He's quite short though

They all look the same in the dark

Text Message | Send

Dad

We are leaving 4 restaurant now, shall we meet you there?

Yeah sorry, Sarah's still getting ready. Taking ages.

Remember. If a girl ever asks you to help put her necklace on, you are morally bound to kiss her on the neck

Thank you wise master

Text Message   Send

Mum

Have a Hershey kiss.

Mum that is a shit.

What? It looks like Hershey's. I don't have my glasses.

TEXT SPEAK

Text Message   Send

Mum

I see you're getting the hang of these emojis

There's too many of them. By the time I'm done looking at them I forget how I feel

Text Message   Send

Mum

> Puuuuu mum what is that smell?

> Please don't tell me that's dinner, lol

Your father burnt his penis in the microwave

> Burnt his penis?

what the heck burnt pcorn

> Pcorn? You mean popcorn?

yes pcorn

> OMG mum then write popcorn! Laughing hard

Text Message | Send

Mum

Let me know when you can shit chat

Haha shit chat?

Brain isn't working I actually typed that! Chit chat

Lol you mean it wasn't even an autocorrect?

Nope I typed shit

And then I thought that doesn't seem right

Mum is losing her noodle

Text Message   Send

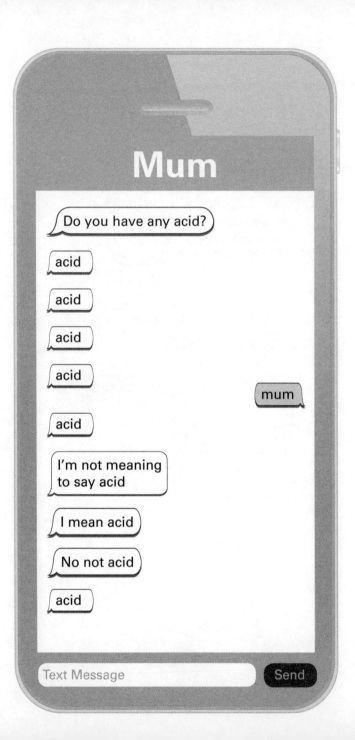

Mum

Hey sweetie, you know that shirt you have that says "LMFAO" on it?

Yeah . . . why?

What does LMFAO mean?

Uhhhmmm . . . Laughing my Fricking Acne Off.

Why would they name their band that?

. . .

Text Message   Send

Mum
OMFG I just died
Allie, what does ‘omfg’ mean?
Dude u should no. duhh
This is your mother.
Oh my fried grapes . . . I thought it was obvious.
Oh well okay then.
Text Message
Send

Mum

I watched Annie Hall
again last night. LMAO

Do you even know
what that means?

It's like haha right?

It means laughing
my ass off . . .

Oh no!

Text Message   Send

Mum

Hey quick question. Can you teach me how to make that penis from symbols in a text?

umm? you really want me to show u how to make a penis?

Yeah, it looks like ===D or something . . .

8===D

I don't even want to know.

Text Message   Send

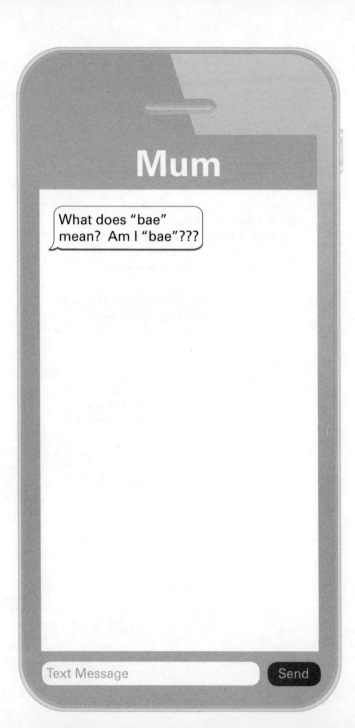

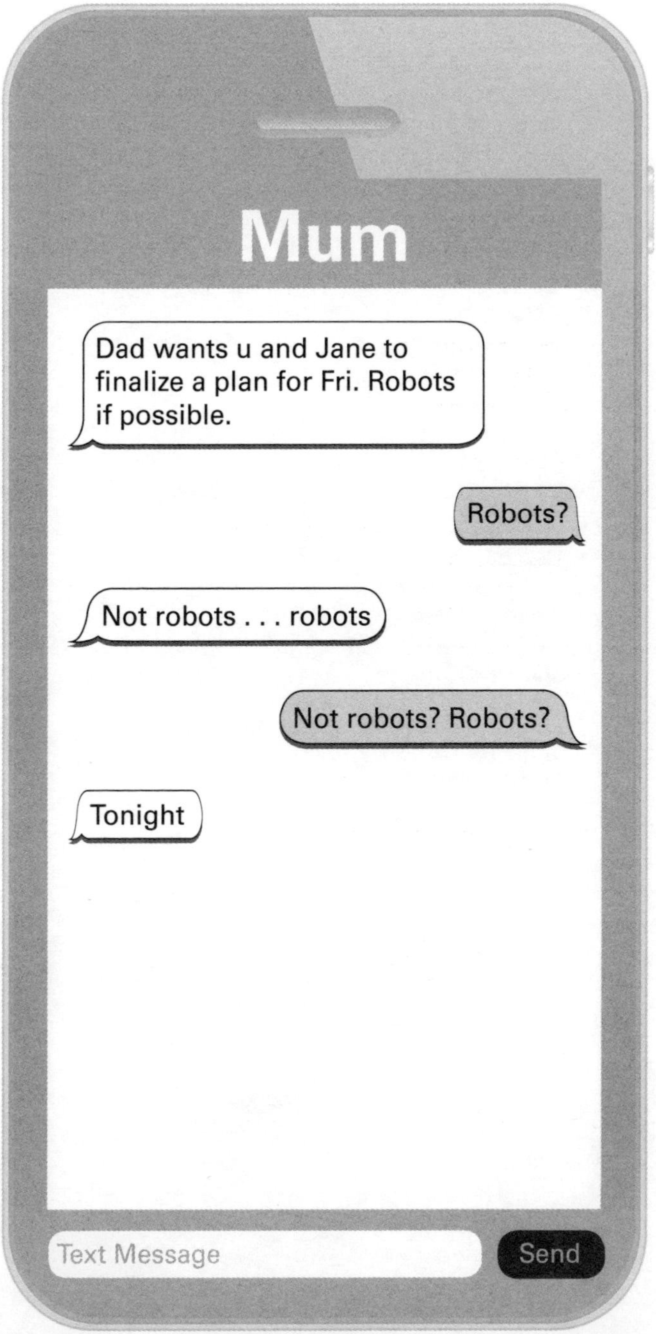
Mum
Dad wants u and Jane to finalize a plan for Fri. Robots if possible.
Robots?
Not robots . . . robots
Not robots? Robots?
Tonight
Text Message
Send

TOO MUCH INFORMATION

Tell mum to check her email . . .

please . . . ;)

OK. Gimme about 15 min. She's taking anal right now.

anal huh . . .

Hahahah . . . the magic of the iPhone autospell correction!!!

Make that "a nap"

HAHAHAHAHAHAH!

Text Message

Send

WHY PARENTS SHOULD (STILL) NEVER TEXT

Dad

you there shawn

Yea what up daddy-o

i am eating your mother out tonight at 7 so you have to find your own dinner

Not sure how to response to that. Uh, have fun?

i'm not eating her out, i'm eating her out

Oh that clears it up

i mean taking. well this has been a fun chat

Text Message   Send

Mum

dad and I fondled ourselves for the first time last night

we didn't get good results. nothing came up

LMAO mum I don't know what you tried to write but that is hilarious!!

!!! damn auto erect !!!

Auto Correct!!! We googled ourselves! No results!!!

Text Message   Send

WHY PARENTS SHOULD (STILL) NEVER TEXT

Mum

Hey mum! The crack I bought for dad's birthday was about five hundred, that okay?

Wow! It was so much cheaper when I was young!

*cake sorry mum

Wait what? Mum? o____o

Text Message   Send

Mum

Do you still need help sewing? I can come over on Sunday.

No – I urinated my pants today.

I urinated my pants.

I heard you. Why?? Are you ok?

I am trying to say un hemmed! I did not pee myself!

Phew I was worried for a sec.

Text Message | Send

Mum

> meh. still feel like crap ☹

Have u tried taking some dicks? OMG VICKS!! HAVE YOU TAKEN SOME VICKS!!!

> omg mum!! Im am LMFAO –ing rite now ^.^

yea yea just don't tell your father about this.

Text Message   Send

Mum

I am soooo drunk at Rick and Colleen's right now listening to sooo funny ball stories right now! Pistachios

Text Message   Send

Dad
Lshidmtamsfo. Do you know what that means?
Laughing so hard I dropped my taco and my sombrero fell off. BOOM
BEST. DAD. EVER
Text Message
Send

Mum

Hey Rhys, just telling you that dad has a bent penis. Love you.

Uhm . . . ? Why did you tell me that mum?

Has angers penis

Answers poems

This is terrible. My phone changed it! I meant dad has ambers pens!

Text Message   Send

WHY PARENTS SHOULD (STILL) NEVER TEXT

Mum

Hey Em do you have my masturbator? Can't find it. Thought I gave it to your daddy, but he says he only has his. Did I let u use it for something?

It's going to be hard, but I'm just gonna pretend like I never saw this

I meant MasterCard. Do you have my MasterCard? That's embarrassing. L-O-L

I'm dying.

Text Message   Send

Mum

Hi Dan guess what?
The deer are back in the yard!
I just fed one of them out of my vagina
Ignore last sentence!
I just fed one of the deer out of my vagina
Out on my V E R A N D A my phone wont let me spell it

Lol be careful mum

Text Message   Send

Mum
How's Uncle Dick getting to the reception?
Dick is coming in my vulva. Dick is in my vulva!
Uhhh . . .
Dicks's coming in my vulva at 7
VOLVO mom? lol.
YES VUVLVA
Text Message
Send